Comparing Data

Tessa Patel

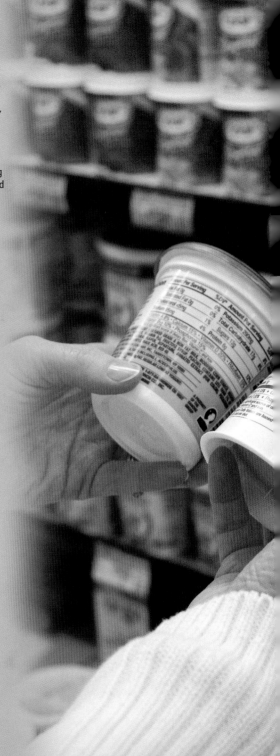

PICTURE CREDITS
Cover, 11, 14–15, Gaston Vanzet; 1, 7 (right), 9 (below), APL/Corbis; 2, 8, 10, 16, Photolibrary.com; 4 (above right), 5 (right), Ibis for Kids Australia; 4 (below right), Marmaduke St. John/Alamy; 6, Michael Newman/PhotoEdit, Inc.; 7 (left), 12, Tony Freeman/PhotoEdit, Inc.; 9 (above), Liane Cary/age fotostock; 18–19 (all), 21, Getty Images.

Produced through the worldwide resources of the National Geographic Society, John M. Fahey, Jr., President and Chief Executive Officer; Gilbert M. Grosvenor, Chairman of the Board; Nina D. Hoffman, Executive Vice President and President, Books and Education Publishing Group.

PREPARED BY NATIONAL GEOGRAPHIC SCHOOL PUBLISHING
Steve Mico, Executive Vice President and Publisher, Children's Books and Education Publishing Group; Marianne Hiland, Editor in Chief; Lynnette Brent, Executive Editor; Michael Murphy and Barbara Wood, Senior Editors; Nicole Rouse, Editor; Bea Jackson, Design Director; David Dumo, Art Director; Shanin Glenn, Designer; Margaret Sidlosky, Illustrations Director; Matt Wascavage, Manager of Publishing Services; Sean Philpotts, Production Manager.

MANUFACTURING AND QUALITY MANAGEMENT
Christopher A. Liedel, Chief Financial Officer; Phillip L. Schlosser, Vice President; Clifton M. Brown III, Director.

BOOK DEVELOPMENT
Ibis for Kids Australia Pty Limited.

Published by the National Geographic Society
1145 17th Street, N.W.
Washington, D.C. 20036-4688

Product No. 4W1005067

ISBN-13: 978-1-4263-5063-4
ISBN-10: 1-4263-5063-5

2010 2009 2008 2007 2006
1 2 3 4 5 6 7 8 9 10 11 12 13 14 15

Printed in China

Contents

Our picture graph shows how we come to school.

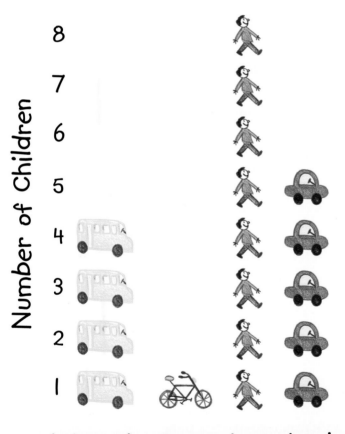

Ways to Come to School

4

All of these pictures show numbers. What do the numbers tell us?

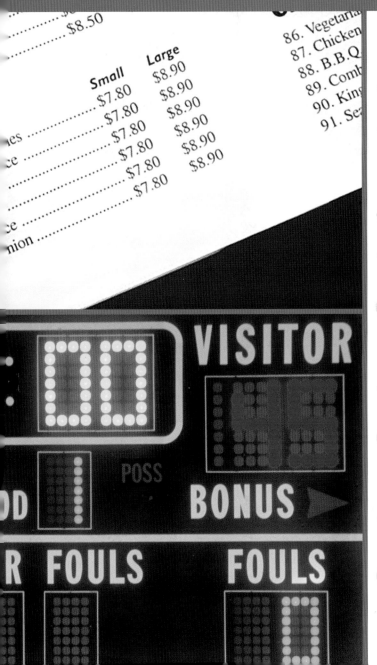

$8.50

	Small	Large
	$7.80	$8.90
...es	$7.80	$8.90
...ce	$7.80	$8.90
	$7.80	$8.90
	$7.80	$8.90
...ce	$7.80	$8.90
...nion	$7.80	

86. Vegetaria...
87. Chicken...
88. B.B.Q...
89. Comb...
90. King...
91. Se...

VISITOR

POSS

BONUS ▶

OD

R FOULS   FOULS

Today
Partly cloudy and windy.
Highs: 52° to 59°
Lows: 30° to 42°

Thursday
Partly cloudy; slight chance of showers.
Highs: 52° to 59°
Lows: 33° to 43°

Friday
Mostly cloudy with a chance of showers.
Highs: 52° to 59°
Lows: 30° to 42°

Saturday
Mostly cloudy; isolated storms.
Highs: 52° to 59°
Lows: 30° to 42°

Sunday
Mostly cloudy with a chance of showers.
Highs: 52° to 59°
Lows: 30° to 42°

Collecting Data

We collect information to learn things. This information is called **data**. We can collect data about many different things.

Data can be information about money. These people are counting money they collected.

Data can be information about weather. This boy is using a thermometer to see what the **temperature** is.

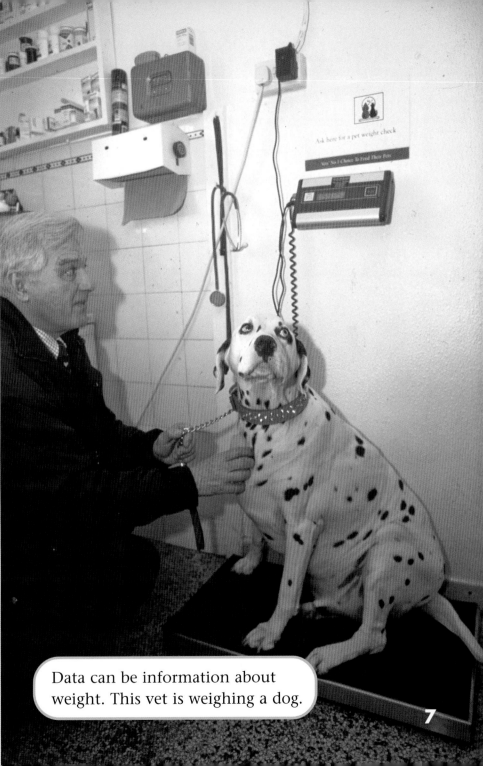

Data can be information about weight. This vet is weighing a dog.

Numbers Show Data

People use data every day. Often this information is shown in numbers.

Numbers can show how much a container holds.

Aspendell 12

North Lake 14
Lake Sabrina 14
South Lake 17

Numbers can show how many miles it is from one place to another.

TIGERS QTR. GUEST
14 4 28

DOWN YDS. TO GO BALL ON
1 10 33

Numbers can show the **score** at a game.

Tables and Graphs

Sometimes people want to compare data. We can compare by putting data in a **table** or a **graph**. This table and bar graph are about the **speeds** of different animals.

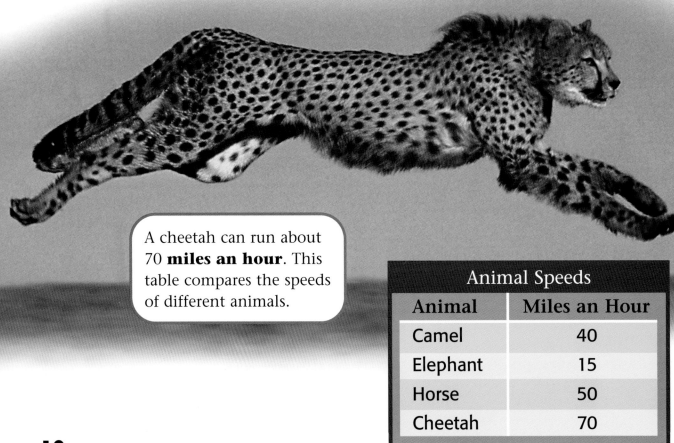

A cheetah can run about 70 **miles an hour**. This table compares the speeds of different animals.

Animal Speeds	
Animal	**Miles an Hour**
Camel	40
Elephant	15
Horse	50
Cheetah	70

Animal Speeds

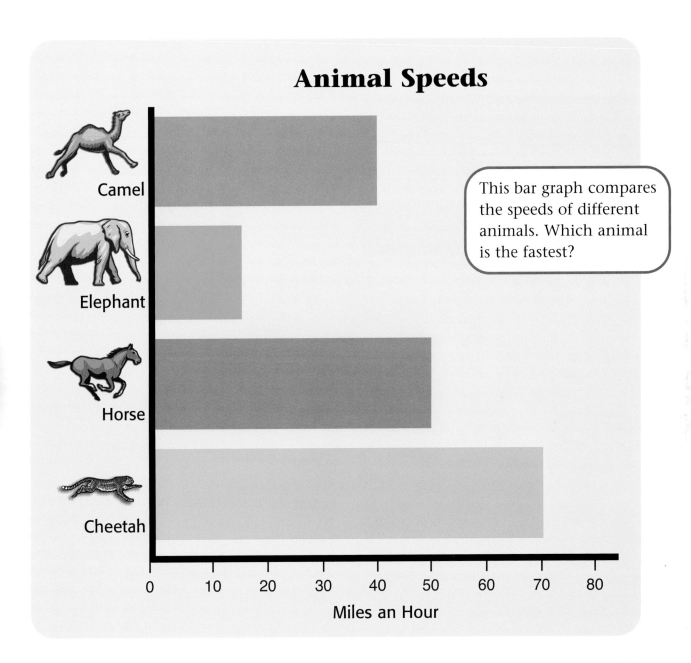

This bar graph compares the speeds of different animals. Which animal is the fastest?

Camel

Elephant

Horse

Cheetah

0   10   20   30   40   50   60   70   80

Miles an Hour

This table and bar graph are about the heights of different plants.

Plant Height	
Plant	**Inches**
Plant 1	8
Plant 2	10
Plant 3	9

This boy is measuring the plants to find out which one is the tallest.

Plant Height

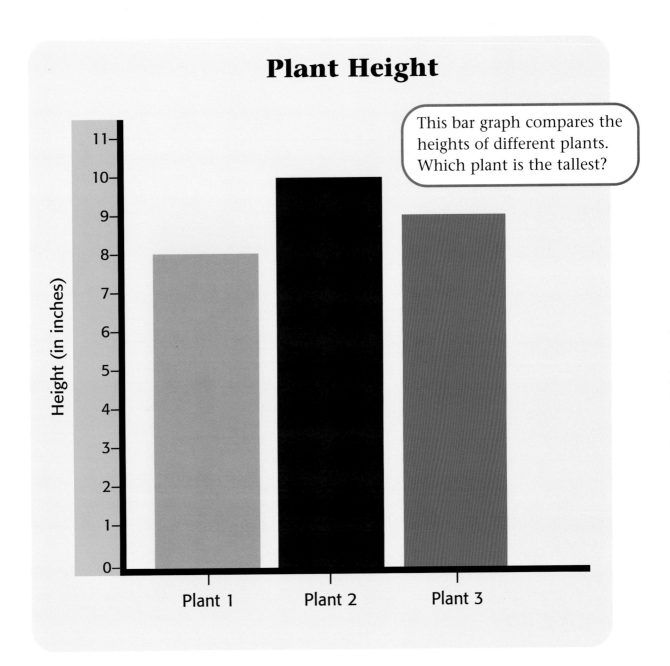

This bar graph compares the heights of different plants. Which plant is the tallest?

Data Showing Amounts

Data can be information about things we count. We can show this kind of information in graphs, too.

Ten students voted for their favorite kind of juice. This circle graph shows how many students like each kind.

Favorite Juices

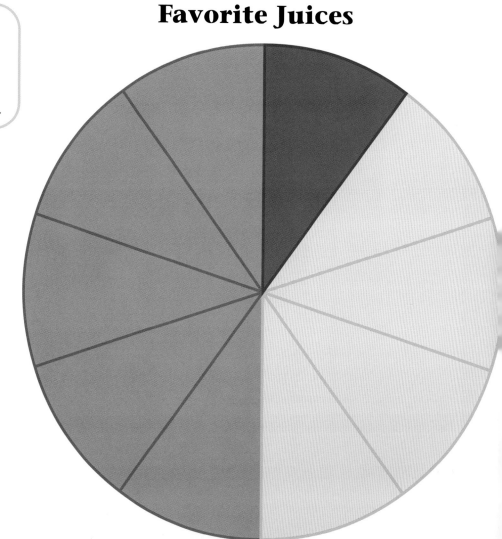

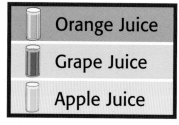

Orange Juice

Grape Juice

Apple Juice

Favorite Juices

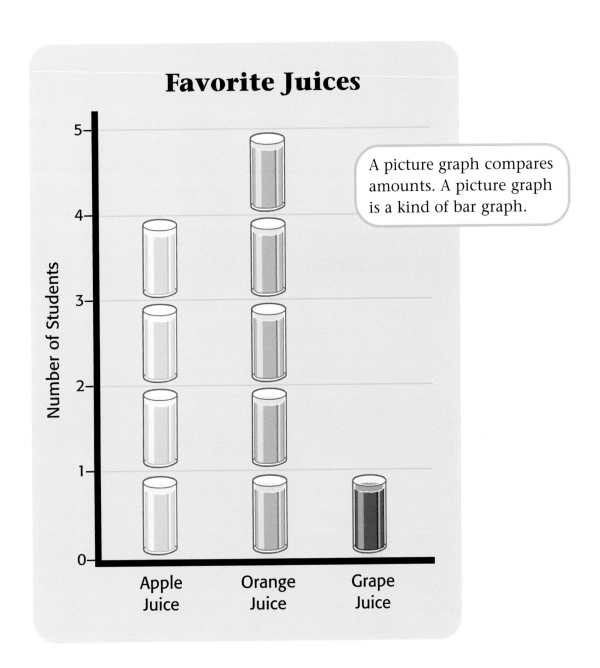

A picture graph compares amounts. A picture graph is a kind of bar graph.

Data Showing Change

We can use data to show how things have changed over time. Sometimes we show data about change in a graph. We can also show data about change in a table.

Tim's Growth	
Age (in years)	Height (in inches)
3	34
5	40
7	45
9	50

This table has data about Tim's height. It shows his height from ages 3 to 9.

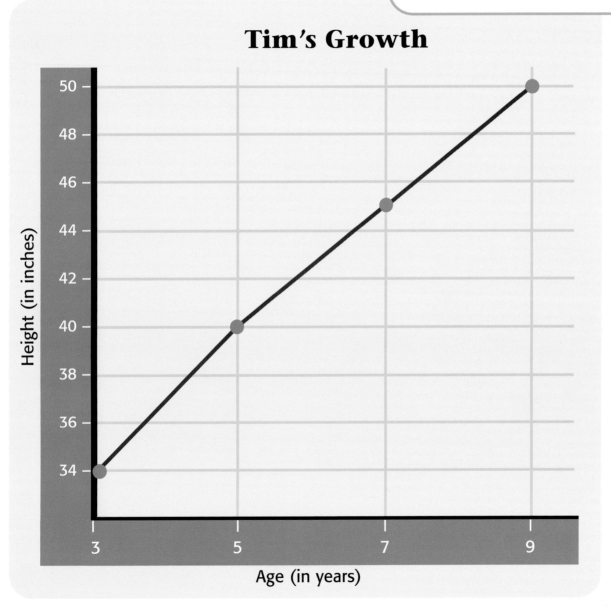

A line graph shows change. The dots show data from the table.

Tim's Growth

Height (in inches) — vertical axis: 34, 36, 38, 40, 42, 44, 46, 48, 50

Age (in years) — horizontal axis: 3, 5, 7, 9

Amazing Data!

We can use data to compare things that are bigger than usual. A normal hot dog is about 6 inches long. Do you know the length of the world's longest hot dog?

This ice cream cake weighs nearly 11,000 pounds!

This enchilada is about 10 feet wide. It weighs more than 800 pounds!

This hot dog is more than 16 feet long!

19

Favorite Sports

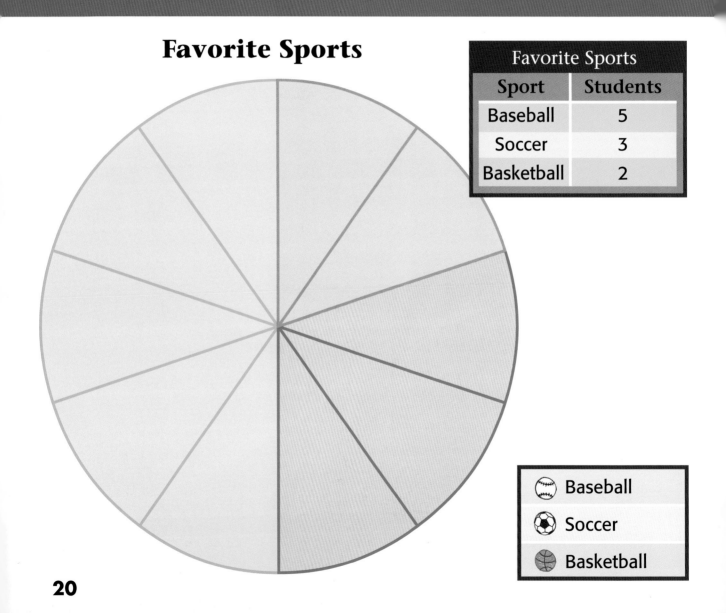

Favorite Sports	
Sport	Students
Baseball	5
Soccer	3
Basketball	2

Baseball

Soccer

Basketball

Talk about the data shown on this page.
What comparisons can you make?

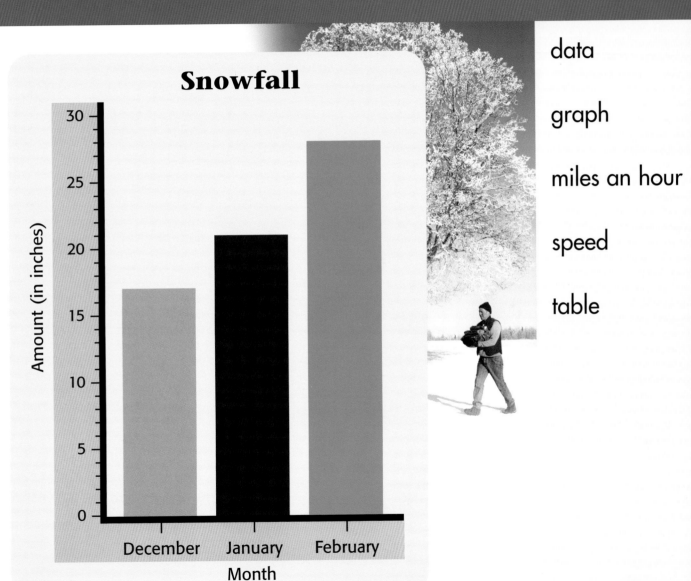

Snowfall

Amount (in inches)

30
25
20
15
10
5
0

December   January   February

Month

data

graph

miles an hour

speed

table

Glossary

data (page 6)
Information
We can collect data about different topics.

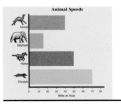

graph (page 10)
A drawing used to show and compare data
We can use a graph to compare the speeds of animals.

miles an hour (page 10)
A measurement of speed that tells how many miles something travels in one hour
A cheetah can run about 70 miles an hour.

score (page 9)
The number of points made in a game
The score of a baseball game is a kind of data.

KEY CONCEPT

speed (page 10)
How fast something travels
Some horses can run at a speed of 50 miles an hour.

KEY CONCEPT

table (page 10)
Information shown in columns and rows
We can use a table to show data.

Animal Speeds	
Animal	Miles an Hour
Camel	40
Elephant	15
Horse	50
Cheetah	70

temperature (page 7)
How hot or cold something is
Sometimes people collect data about temperature.

Index